The Salvation Novena

An Advent Novena Scriptural Rosary

Larry London

Our Sunday Visitor Publishing Division
Our Sunday Visitor, Inc.
Huntington, Indiana 46750

Nihil Obstat
Rev. Charles R. Dautremont, Censor of Books
Imprimatur
Rev. Msgr. Terrence L. Stewart, Vicar General
October 2, 1996
The *nihil obstat* and *imprimatur* are official declarations
that a book or pamphlet is free of doctrinal or moral error.
No implication is contained therein that those who have
granted the *nihil obstat* and *imprimatur* agree with the
content, opinions, or statements expressed.

ISBN: 0-87973-917-7
LCCN: 97-66784
Illustrations by: Robert F. McGovern
Cover design by: Monica Watts
PRINTED IN THE UNITED STATES OF AMERICA
917

INTRODUCTION

In the beginning God created a world of peace and harmony that He found to be very good. But after the original sin of our first parents, the world changed dramatically. Their disobedience caused the family of man to be separated from God, and without living in God's grace, the world was soon full of every wickedness and evil.

That was by no means to be the end of the story, for in His great love, God did not abandon mankind but rather promised a Savior who would heal the rift and bridge the great chasm between God and man. God would one day provide the means for those who were open to receive His truth, to enter into His family.

The Scriptures reveal a story of hope upon hope to those who would eagerly await a world of righteousness where God's will is paramount. The Old Testament records the many promises of salvation which flowed freely over the centuries as those who strove for righteousness eagerly awaited their Redeemer. But the Bible also reveals the great pain, anguish, and emptiness experienced by all those who struggled in this world of tears. Surely, for anyone with eyes to see, mankind was, and is, in desperate need of the Savior.

It is this wondrous and universal story of the longing and hope experienced from the promises of salvation that pours forth from the Scriptures, which *The Salvation Novena: an Advent Scriptural Rosary* centers upon. It is a story, and a hope, for everyone, not only for the past, but for the present and the future. Each of us, regardless of the day, are asked to long for righteousness and then eagerly open our hearts to salvation in welcoming into our lives the King of Glory. It is a story which will not reach total fulfillment until the end of time when our Lord Jesus returns, and therefore, this meditation also looks forward to that time of His Second Coming in glory.

And so through praying the Salvation Novena Scriptural Rosary with our Blessed Mother, we hope to come to a greater appreciation for that which Almighty God has wrought for us through the Savior in His plan of salvation. Let us then pray that each person who experiences this novena will come to know, love, and serve the

Lord more completely for the glory of the One to whom we owe everything!

This novena may fittingly be prayed at any time but is especially appropriate during the Advent Season. During the days of this novena would be an excellent time to take advantage of the Sacrament of Reconciliation.

Each Scripture passage has been divided with a slash (/) so that it may easily be proclaimed in a two-part fashion, as is common when the Rosary is prayed by more than one person. Praying a novena in a group setting is in itself quite Scripturally sound. The first novena was prayed in a group setting by the Apostles, Mary, and those who were gathered in the upper room during those nine days after the Lord ascended into heaven while they awaited the promised Holy Spirit.

May the Blessed Virgin show us, through these Scripture meditations, the way to her Son, who is the source of all good things. Amen.

The Mysteries

THE GENESIS
MYSTERIES

*A*lmighty God, please help me to understand
the great loss that man experienced when he
first disobeyed you. Let me understand the grave
seriousness of sin and all the pain and sorrow that
man has brought upon himself. Most of all, dear

Lord, help my understanding of sin and its many consequences and build up my resolve to obey you.

In the name of the Father, and of the Son, and of the Holy Spirit. Amen.

First Genesis Mystery
The Creation

✤*Our Father*✤

In the beginning, when God created the heavens and the earth, /

. . . a mighty wind swept over the waters.

Genesis 1:12

✤*Hail Mary*✤

Then God said: "Let us make man in our image, after our likeness. /

Let them have dominion over . . . all the creatures. . . ."

Genesis 1:26

✤*Hail Mary*✤

The Lord God formed man out of the clay of the ground and blew into his nostrils the breath of life, /

and so man became a living being.

Genesis 2:7

✤*Hail Mary*✤

Then the Lord God planted a garden in Eden, in
    the east, /
and he placed there the man whom he had formed.

Genesis 2:8

✤*Hail Mary*✤

God created man in his image;
    in the divine image he created him; /
    male and female he created them.

Genesis 1:27

✤*Hail Mary*✤

God blessed them, saying: "Be fertile and
    multiply; /
fill the earth and subdue it."

Genesis 1:28

✤*Hail Mary*✤

Out of the ground the Lord God made various
    trees grow that were delightful to look at and
    good for food, /
with the tree of life in the middle of the garden
    and the tree of the knowledge of good and
    bad.

Genesis 2:9

✤*Hail Mary*✤

The Lᴏʀᴅ God gave man this order: "You are free
to eat from any of the trees of the garden /
except the tree of knowledge of good and bad. . . ."

Genesis 2:16-17

✤Hail Mary✤

"From that tree you shall not eat; /
the moment you eat from it you are surely
doomed to die."

Genesis 2:17

✤Hail Mary✤

God looked at everything he had made, /
and he found it very good.

Genesis 1:31

✤Hail Mary✤

✤Glory Be✤

Second Genesis Mystery
The Original Sin

✤Our Father✤

The woman answered the serpent; "We may eat
of the fruit of the trees in the garden; /
it is only about the fruit of the tree in the middle
of the garden that God said, 'You shall not

10

eat it or even touch it, lest you die.' ”

Genesis 3:2-3

✤Hail Mary✤

But the serpent said to the woman: “You
    certainly will not die! /

No. God knows well that the moment you eat of
    it your eyes will be opened and you will be
    like gods who know what is good and what
    is bad.”

Genesis 3:4-5

✤Hail Mary✤

The woman saw that the tree was good for food,
    pleasing to the eyes, and desirable for
    gaining wisdom. /

So she took some of its fruit and ate it; and she
    also gave some to her husband, who was
    with her, and he ate it.

Genesis 3:6

✤Hail Mary✤

Then the eyes of both of them were opened, and
    they realized that they were naked; /

so they sewed fig leaves together and made
    loincloths for themselves.

Genesis 3:7

✤*Hail Mary*✤

When they heard the sound of the Lord God
moving about in the garden at the breezy
time of the day, /
the man and his wife hid themselves from the
Lord God among the trees of the garden.

Genesis 3:8

✤*Hail Mary*✤

The Lord God then called the man and asked
him, /
"Where are you?"

Genesis 3:9

✤*Hail Mary*✤

He answered, "I heard you in the garden; /
but I was afraid, because I was naked, so I hid
myself."

Genesis 3:10

✤*Hail Mary*✤

Then he asked, "Who told you that you were
naked? /
You have eaten, then, from the tree of which I
had forbidden you to eat!"

Genesis 3:11

✤*Hail Mary*✤

The man replied, "the woman whom you put
    here with me — /
she gave me fruit from the tree, and so I ate it."

Genesis 3:12

✤Hail Mary✤

The LORD God then asked the woman, "Why did
    you do such a thing?" /
The woman answered, "The serpent tricked me
    into it, so I ate it."

Genesis 3:13

✤Hail Mary✤

✤Glory Be✤

Third Genesis Mystery
The Punishment

✤Our Father✤

Then the LORD God said to the serpent:
    "Because you have done this, you shall be
    banned
    from all the animals and from all the wild
    creatures; /
    On your belly shall you crawl,
    and dirt shall you eat all the days of your life."

Genesis 3:14

✤Hail Mary✤

13

"I will put enmity between you and the woman,
   and between your offspring and hers; /
He will strike at your head,
   while you strike at his heel."

Genesis 3:15

✣*Hail Mary*✣

To the woman he said:
"I will intensify the pangs of your childbearing;
   in pain shall you bring forth children. /
Yet your urge shall be for your husband,
   and he shall be your master."

Genesis 3:16

✣*Hail Mary*✣

To the man he said:
"Because you listened to your wife and ate from
   the tree of which I had forbidden you to eat, /
Cursed be the ground because of you!
   In toil shall you eat its yield
   all the days of your life."

Genesis 3:17

✣*Hail Mary*✣

"Thorns and thistles shall it bring forth to you, /
   as you eat of the plants of the field."

Genesis 3:18

✣*Hail Mary*✣

"By the sweat of your face
    shall you get bread to eat, /
Until you return to the ground
    from which you were taken;"

Genesis 3:19

✤Hail Mary✤

"For you are dirt, /
    and to dirt you shall return."

Genesis 3:19

✤Hail Mary✤

The man called his wife Eve, /
because she became the mother of all the living.

Genesis 3:20

✤Hail Mary✤

Then the LORD God said: "See! The man has
    become like one of us, knowing what is
    good and what is bad! /
Therefore, he must not be allowed to put out his
    hand to take fruit from the tree of life also,
    and thus eat of it and live forever."

Genesis 3:22

✤Hail Mary✤

The LORD God therefore banished him from
    the garden of Eden, /

15

to till the ground from which he had been taken.

Genesis 3:23

✤*Hail Mary*✤

✤*Glory Be*✤

Fourth Genesis Mystery
The Firstfruits of Sin

✤*Our Father*✤

The man had relations with his wife Eve, and she conceived and bore Cain. . . . /
Next she bore his brother Abel.

Genesis 4:1-2

✤*Hail Mary*✤

In the course of time Cain brought an offering to the LORD from the fruit of the soil, /
while Abel, for his part, brought one of the best firstlings of his flock.

Genesis 4:3-4

✤*Hail Mary*✤

The LORD looked with favor on Abel and his offering, but on Cain and his offering he did not. /
Cain greatly resented this and was crestfallen.

Genesis 4:4-5

✤*Hail Mary*✤

Cain said to his brother Abel, "Let us go out in the field." /

When they were in the field, Cain attacked his brother Abel and killed him.

Genesis 4:8

✤*Hail Mary*✤

Then the LORD asked Cain, "Where is your brother Abel?" /

He answered, "I do not know. Am I my brother's keeper?"

Genesis 4:9

✤*Hail Mary*✤

The LORD then said: "What have you done! / Listen: Your brother's blood cries out to me from the soil!"

Genesis 4:10

✤*Hail Mary*✤

"Therefore you shall be banned from the soil that opened its mouth to receive your brother's blood from your hand. . . ." /

Cain then left the Lord's presence and settled in the land of Nod, east of Eden.

Genesis 4:11, 16

✤*Hail Mary*✤

When the L<small>ORD</small> saw how great was man's
   wickedness on earth. . . . /
he regretted that he had made man on the earth,
   and his heart was grieved.

Genesis 6:5-6

✤*Hail Mary*✤

He said to Noah: "I have decided to put an end to
   all mortals on earth; /
the earth is full of lawlessness because of them."

Genesis 6:13

✤*Hail Mary*✤

"But with you I will establish my covenant; /
   you and your sons, your wife and your
   sons' wives, shall go into the ark."

Genesis 6:18

✤*Hail Mary*✤

✤*Glory Be*✤

Fifth Genesis Mystery
The Universality of Sin

✤*Our Father*✤

The wrath of God is indeed being revealed from
heaven against every impiety and wickedness /
of those who suppress the truth by their
wickedness.

Romans 1:18

✤*Hail Mary*✤

For what can be known about God is evident to
them, /
because God made it evident to them.

Romans 1:19

✤*Hail Mary*✤

Ever since the creation of the world, his invisible
attributes of eternal power and divinity have
been able to be understood and perceived in
what he has made. /
As a result, they have no excuse;

Romans 1:20

✤*Hail Mary*✤

for although they knew God they did not accord
him glory as God or give him thanks. /

19

Instead, they became vain in their reasoning,
and their senseless minds were darkened.

Romans 1:21

✤Hail Mary✤

While claiming to be wise, they became fools. . . . /
They exchanged the truth of God for a lie and
revered and worshiped the creature rather
than the creator, who is blessed forever.
Amen.

Romans 1:22, 25

✤Hail Mary✤

Although they know the just decree of God that
all who practice such things deserve death, /
they not only do them but give approval to those
who practice them.

Romans 1:32

✤Hail Mary✤

All have sinned /
and are deprived of the glory of God.

Romans 3:23

✤Hail Mary✤

Therefore, just as through one person sin entered
the world, and through sin, death, /

and thus death came to all, inasmuch as all
    sinned. . . .

Romans 5:12

✤Hail Mary✤

But death reigned from Adam to Moses, even
    over those who did not sin after the pattern
    of the trespass of Adam, /
who is the type of the one who was to come.

Romans 5:14

✤Hail Mary✤

For just as through the disobedience of one
    person the many were made sinners, /
so through the obedience of one the many will be
    made righteous.

Romans 5:19

✤Hail Mary✤

✤Glory Be✤

THE REMORSEFUL MYSTERIES

*D*ear Lord, help me to see myself as I truly *am* — lost and alone without you! Let me hunger and thirst for you as did your people through the many centuries as they awaited your Anointed One. Reveal to me my sins, Lord, and *show me what I must do to turn to you. Embrace me, my God, for I am alone and my life is empty without you.*

In the name of the Father, and of the Son, and of the Holy Spirit. Amen.

First Remorseful Mystery
Tobit's Prayer

✤*Our Father*✤

Grief-stricken in spirit, I groaned and wept aloud. / then with sobs I began to pray:

Tobit 3:1

✤*Hail Mary*✤

"You are righteous, O LORD, /
  and all your deeds are just;"

Tobit 3:2

✤*Hail Mary*✤

"All your ways are mercy and truth; /
  you are the judge of the world."

Tobit 3:2

✤*Hail Mary*✤

"And now, O LORD, may you be mindful of me,
  and look with favor upon me. /
Punish me not for my sins,

23

nor for my inadvertent offenses,
nor for those of my fathers."

Tobit 3:3

✤*Hail Mary*✤

"They sinned against you,
and disobeyed your commandments. /
So you handed us over to plundering, exile, and
death, . . ."

Tobit 3:3-4

✤*Hail Mary*✤

"we were an object lesson, a byword, a reproach /
in all the nations among whom you scattered us."

Tobit 3-4

✤*Hail Mary*✤

"Yes, your judgments are many and true /
in dealing with me as my sins
and those of my fathers deserve."

Tobit 3:5

✤*Hail Mary*✤

"For we have not kept your commandments, /
nor have we trodden the paths
of truth before you."

Tobit 3:5

✤Hail Mary✤

"So now, deal with me as you please,
and command my life breath to be taken from
    me, /
that I may go from the face of the earth into dust."

Tobit 3:6

✤Hail Mary✤

"LORD, command me to be delivered from such
    anguish; /
let me go to the everlasting abode;
LORD, refuse me not."

Tobit 3:6

✤Hail Mary✤

✤Glory Be✤

Second Remorseful Mystery
Prayer for Salvation

✤Our Father✤

Do not reprove me in your anger, LORD, /
    nor punish me in your wrath.

Psalm 6:2

✤Hail Mary✤

Have pity on me, Lᴏᴅᴀ, for I am weak; /
Psalm 6:3

✤*Hail Mary*✤

heal me, Lᴏᴅᴀ, for my bones are trembling. /
Psalm 6:3

✤*Hail Mary*✤

In utter teror is my soul — /
    and you, Lᴏᴅᴀ, how long. . . ?
Psalm 6:4

✤*Hail Mary*✤

Turn, Lᴏᴅᴀ, save my life; /
    in your mercy rescue me.
Psalm 6:5

✤*Hail Mary*✤

For who among the dead remembers you? /
    Who praises you in Sheol?
Psalm 6:6

✤*Hail Mary*✤

I am wearied with sighing;
    all night long tears drench my bed; /
    my couch is soaked with weeping.
Psalm 6:7

✤*Hail Mary*✤

My eyes are dimmed with sorrow; /
    worn out because of all my foes.

Psalm 6:8

✤Hail Mary✤

Away from me, all who do evil! /
    The L<small>ORD</small> has heard my weeping.

Psalm 6:9

✤Hail Mary✤

The L<small>ORD</small> has heard my prayer; /
    the L<small>ORD</small> takes up my plea.

Psalm 6:10

✤Hail Mary✤

✤Glory Be✤

Third Remorseful Mystery
The Sinner's Prayer

✤Our Father✤

L<small>ORD</small>, punish me no more in your anger; /
    in your wrath do not chastise me!

Psalm 38:2

✤Hail Mary✤

Your arrows have sunk deep in me, /

27

your hand has come down upon me.

Psalm 38:3

✤*Hail Mary*✤

My flesh is afflicted because of your anger; /
  my frame aches because of my sin.

Psalm 38:4

✤*Hail Mary*✤

My iniquities overwhelmed me; /
  a burden, beyond my strength.

Psalm 38:5

✤*Hail Mary*✤

I am stooped and deeply bowed; /
  all day I go about mourning.

Psalm 38:7

✤*Hail Mary*✤

I am numbed and utterly crushed; /
  I wail with anguish of heart.

Psalm 38:9

✤*Hail Mary*✤

LORD, I wait for you; /
  O LORD my God, answer me.

Psalm 38:16

✤*Hail Mary*✤

I am very near to falling, /
 and my pain is with me always.

Psalm 38:18

❧Hail Mary❧

I acknowledge my guilt /
 and grieve over my sin.

Psalm 38:19

❧Hail Mary❧

Forsake me not, O LORD; /
 my God, be not far from me!

Psalm 38:22

❧Hail Mary❧

❧Glory Be❧

Fourth Remorseful Mystery
The Repentance Prayer

✤*Our Father*✤

Have mercy on me, O God, in your goodness; /
  In the greatness of your compassion wipe
  out my offense.

Psalm 51:3

✤*Hail Mary*✤

Thoroughly wash me from my guilt /
  and of my sin cleanse me.

Psalm 51:4

✤*Hail Mary*✤

For I acknowledge my offense, /
  and my sin is before me always;

Psalm 51:5

✤*Hail Mary*✤

"Against you only have I sinned,
  and done what is evil in your sight"— /
That you may be justified in your sentence,
  vindicated when you condemn.

Psalm 51:6

✤*Hail Mary*✤

Indeed, in guilt was I born, /

and in sin my mother conceived me;
Psalm 51:7

✤*Hail Mary*✤

Cleanse me of sin with hyssop, that I may be
    purified; /
    wash me, and I shall be whiter than snow.
Psalm 51:9

✤*Hail Mary*✤

Turn away your face from my sins, /
    and blot out all of my guilt.
Psalm 51:11

✤*Hail Mary*✤

A clean heart create for me, O God, /
    and a steadfast spirit renew within me.
Psalm 51:12

✤*Hail Mary*✤

Cast me not out from your presence, /
    and your holy spirit take not from me.
Psalm 51:13

✤*Hail Mary*✤

Give me back the joy of your salvation, /
    and a willing spirit sustain in me.
Psalm 51:14

✤*Hail Mary*✤

✤*Glory Be*✤

Fifth Remorseful Mystery
God's Forgiveness

✤*Our Father*✤

Into your hands I commend my spirit; /
    you will redeem me, O LORD, O faithful God.

                    Psalms 31:6

✤*Hail Mary*✤

How great is the goodness, O LORD,
    which you have in store for those who fear
    you, /
And which, toward those who take refuge in you,
    you show in the sight of men.

                    Psalm 31:20

✤*Hail Mary*✤

Once I said in my anguish,
    "I am cut off from your sight" /
Yet you heard the sound of my pleading
    when I cried out to you.

                    Psalm 31:23

✤*Hail Mary*✤

Happy is he whose fault is taken away, /
    whose sin is covered.

Psalm 32:1

✣*Hail Mary*✣

Happy the man to whom the Lᴏʀᴅ imputes not
        guilt, /
in whose spirit there is no guile.

Psalm 32:2

✣*Hail Mary*✣

As long as I would not speak, /
    my bones wasted away
    with my groaning all the day,

Psalm 32:3

✣*Hail Mary*✣

For day and night your hand was heavy upon me; /
    my strength was dried up as by the heat of
    summer.

Psalm 32:4

✣*Hail Mary*✣

Then I acknowledged my sin to you,
    my guilt I covered not. /
I said, "I confess my faults to the Lᴏʀᴅ,"
    and you took away the guilt of my sin.

Psalm 32:5

✣*Hail Mary*✣

For this shall every faithful man pray to you in
time of stress. /
Though deep waters overflow,
they shall not reach him.

Psalm 32:6

✣*Hail Mary*✣

Many are the sorrows of the wicked, /
but kindness surrounds him
who trusts in the LORD.

Psalm 32:10

✣*Hail Mary*✣

✣*Glory Be*✣

THE ANCIENT MYSTERIES

*L*ord God, strengthen me that, like Abraham,
I may grow to have faith that trusts totally
in you and your Word. Help me be confident like
David as I long for you and your revelation to the
world. And as I seek to know you more fully, let

my lips also proclaim your praises and so give
hope to those around me, as did your servants of old.

    In the name of the Father, and of the Son, and
of the Holy Spirit. Amen.

First Ancient Mystery
The Promise of Faith

✤*Our Father*✤

Some time after these events, God put Abraham
    to the test. . . . /
"Take your son Isaac . . . go to the land of
    Moriah. There you shall offer him up as a
    holocaust. . . ."

Genesis 22:1-2

✤*Hail Mary*✤

Thereupon Abraham took the wood for the
    holocaust and laid it on his son Isaac's
    shoulders, /
while he himself carried the fire and the knife.

Genesis 22:6

✤*Hail Mary*✤

When they came to the place of which God had
    told him, Abraham built an altar there and

arranged the wood on it. /
Next he tied up his son Isaac, and put him on top
    of the wood on the altar.

Genesis 22:9

✤Hail Mary✤

Then he reached out /
    and took the knife to slaughter his son.

Genesis 22:10

✤Hail Mary✤

But the LORD's messenger called to him from
    heaven, /
"Abraham, Abraham!" "Yes, LORD,"
    he answered.

Genesis 22:11

✤Hail Mary✤

"Do not lay your hand on the boy," said the
    messenger. "Do not do the least thing to him. /
I know now how devoted you are to God, since
    you did not withhold from me your own
    beloved son."

Genesis 22:12

✤Hail Mary✤

As Abraham looked about, he spied a ram caught
    by its horns in the thicket. /

37

So he went and took the ram and offered it up as a holocaust in place of his son.

Genesis 22:13

✤*Hail Mary*✤

. . . "I swear by myself, declares the LORD, that because you acted as you did /

in not withholding from me your beloved son, I will bless you abundantly . . ."

Genesis 22:16-17

✤*Hail Mary*✤

"and make your descendants as countless as the stars of the sky and the sands of the seashore; /

your descendants shall take possession of the gates of their enemies,"

Genesis 22:17

✤*Hail Mary*✤

"and in your descendants all the nations of the earth shall find blessing — /

all this because you obeyed my command."

Genesis 22:18

✤*Hail Mary*✤

✤*Glory Be*✤

Second Ancient Mystery
The Promises of Old

✤*Our Father*✤

God replied: "Nevertheless, your wife Sarah is to
bear you a son, and you shall call him Isaac. /
I will maintain my covenant with him as an
everlasting pact, to be his God and the God
of his descendants after him."

Genesis 17:19

✤*Hail Mary*✤

"The scepter shall never depart from Judah,
or the mace from between his legs, /
While tribute is brought to him,
and he receives the peoples' homage."

Genesis 49:10

✤*Hail Mary*✤

I see him, though not now;
I behold him, though not near: /
A star shall advance from Jacob,
and a staff shall rise from Israel.

Numbers 24:17

✤*Hail Mary*✤

"A prophet like me will the LORD, your God, raise

up for you from among your own kinsmen; /
to him you shall listen."

Deuteronomy 18:15

✤*Hail Mary*✤

". . . and will put my words into his mouth; /
he shall tell them all that I command him."

Deuteronomy 18:18

✤*Hail Mary*✤

"If any man will not listen to my words which he
speaks in my name, /
I myself will make him answer for it."

Deuteronomy 18:19

✤*Hail Mary*✤

"The LORD puts to death and gives life; /
he casts down to the nether world;
he raises up again."

1 Samuel 2:6

✤*Hail Mary*✤

"The LORD makes poor and makes rich, /
he humbles, he also exalts."

1 Samuel 2:7

✤*Hail Mary*✤

"He raises the needy from the dust;
from the ash heap he lifts up the poor, /

To seat them with nobles
and make a glorious throne their heritage."

1 Samuel 2:8

✤Hail Mary✤

". . . The Most High in heaven thunders;
the LORD judges the ends of the earth. /
Now may he give strength to his king,
and exalt the horn of his anointed!"

1 Samuel 2:10

✤Hail Mary✤

✤Glory Be✤

Third Ancient Mystery
The Promise of David

✤Our Father✤

"Now then, speak thus to my servant David,
The LORD of hosts has this to say: /
It was I who took you from the pasture and from
the care of the flock to be commander of my
people Israel."

2 Samuel 7:8

✤Hail Mary✤

"I have been with you wherever you went,

and I have destroyed all your enemies before you. /
And I will make you famous like the great ones
    of the earth."

2 Samuel 7:9

✤*Hail Mary*✤

"I will fix a place for my people Israel; /
I will plant them so that they may dwell in their
    place without further disturbance."

2 Samuel 7:10

✤*Hail Mary*✤

". . . I will give you rest from all your enemies. /
The Lord also reveals to you that he will
    establish a house for you."

2 Samuel 7:11

✤*Hail Mary*✤

"And when your time comes and you rest with
    your ancestors, I will raise up your heir after
    you, /
sprung from your loins, and I will make his
    kingdom firm."

2 Samuel 7:12

✤*Hail Mary*✤

"It is he who shall build a house for my name. /
And I will make his royal throne firm forever."

2 Samuel 7:13

✤*Hail Mary*✤

"I will be a father to him, /
    and he shall be a son to me."

2 Samuel 7:14

✤*Hail Mary*✤

". . . but I will not withdraw my favor from him as I
    withdrew it from your predecessor Saul, /
    whom I removed from my presence."

2 Samuel 7:15

✤*Hail Mary*✤

"Your house and your kingdom shall endure
    forever before me; /
your throne shall stand firm forever."

2 Samuel 7:16

✤*Hail Mary*✤

Then King David went in and sat before the Lord
    and said, /
"Who am I, Lord GOD, and who are the members
    of my house, that you have brought me to
    this point?"

2 Samuel 7:18

✤*Hail Mary*✤

✤*Glory Be*✤

Fourth Ancient Mystery
David's Song of Thanksgiving

✤*Our Father*✤

"O LORD, my rock, my fortress, my deliverer, /
  my God, my rock of refuge!"

2 Samuel 22:2-3

✤*Hail Mary*✤

"My shield, the horn of my salvation,
  my stronghold, my refuge, /
  my savior, from violence you keep me safe."

2 Samuel 22:3

✤*Hail Mary*✤

"In my distress I called upon the LORD
  and cried out to my God; /
From his temple he heard my voice,
  and my cry reached his ears."

2 Samuel 22:7

✤*Hail Mary*✤

"He inclined the heavens and came down, /
  with dark clouds under his feet."

2 Samuel 22:10

✤*Hail Mary*✤

"He reached out from on high and grasped me; /
  he drew me out of the deep waters."

2 Samuel 22:17

✤Hail Mary✤

"He rescued me from my mighty enemy, /
from my foes, who were too powerful for me."

2 Samuel 22:18

✤Hail Mary✤

"He set me free in the open, /
and rescued me, because he loves me."

2 Samuel 22:20

✤Hail Mary✤

"You are my lamp, O LORD! /
O my God, you brighten the darkness about me."

2 Samuel 22:29

✤Hail Mary✤

"The LORD live! And blessed be my Rock! /
Extolled be my God, Rock of my salvation."

2 Samuel 22:47

✤Hail Mary✤

"You who gave great victories to your king
and showed kindness to your anointed, /
to David and his posterity forever."

2 Samuel 22:51

✤Hail Mary✤

✤Glory Be✤

Fifth Ancient Mystery
Tobit's Song of Praise

♣*Our Father*♣

. . . Blessed be God who lives forever, /
    because his kingdom lasts for all ages.

Tobit 13:1

♣*Hail Mary*♣

For he scourges and then has mercy;
    he casts down into the depths of the nether world, /
    and he brings up from the great abyss.
    No one can escape his hand.

Tobit 13:2

♣*Hail Mary*♣

. . . Exalt him before every living being, /
    because he is the LORD our God,
    our Father and God forever.

Tobit 13:4

♣*Hail Mary*♣

When you turn back to him with all your heart,
    to do what is right before him, /
Then he will turn back to you,
    and no longer hide his face from you.

Tobit 13:6

♣*Hail Mary*♣

Praise the LORD for his goodness,
>and bless the King of the ages, /

so that his tent may be rebuilt in you with joy.

Tobit 13:10

✤*Hail Mary*✤

A bright light will shine to all parts of the earth;
>many nations shall come to you from afar. . . /

Bearing in their hands their gifts
>for the King of heaven.

Tobit 13:11

✤*Hail Mary*✤

Every generation shall give joyful praise in you, /
>and shall call you the chosen one,
>>through all ages forever.

Tobit 13:11

✤*Hail Mary*✤

. . . Happy are all the men who shall grieve over you,
>over all your chastisements, /

For they shall rejoice in you
>as they behold all your joy forever.

Tobit 13:14

✤*Hail Mary*✤

Jerusalem shall be rebuilt as his home forever. /
>Happy for me if a remnant of my offspring
>>survive

47

to see your glory and to praise the King of
   heaven!

Tobit 13:16

✤*Hail Mary*✤

The gates of Jerusalem shall sing hymns of
   gladness,
   and all her houses shall cry out, "Alleluia! /
"Blessed be God who has raised you up!
   May he be blessed for all ages!"
For in you they shall praise his holy name
   forever.

Tobit 13:18

✤*Hail Mary*✤

✤*Glory Be*✤

THE WISDOM
MYSTERIES

O my Lord, help me to place all my hope in you and not in the world or persons of the world. Strengthen me that I might accomplish the Father's will faithfully as you always did, even through suffering. And dear Lord, show me how to be mindful not only of the obstacles in my journey but also of the great victory which you have already won.

In the name of the Father, and of the Son, and of the Holy Spirit. Amen.

First Wisdom Mystery
Kingdom of the Messiah

✤*Our Father*✤

The kings of the earth rise up,
>   and the princes conspire together
>   against the LORD and against his anointed: /
"Let us break their fetters
>   and cast their bonds from us!"

Psalm 2:2-3

✤*Hail Mary*✤

He who is throned in heaven laughs; /
>   the Lord derides them.

Psalm 2:4

✤*Hail Mary*✤

Then in anger he speaks to them; /
>   he terrifies them in his wrath:

Psalm 2:5

✤*Hail Mary*✤

"I myself have set up my king
  on Zion, / my holy mountain."

Psalm 2:6

✤*Hail Mary*✤

I will proclaim the decree of the LORD:
  The Lord said to me, / "You are my son;
  this day I have begotten you."

Psalm 2:7

✤*Hail Mary*✤

"Ask of me and I will give you the nations for an
  inheritance /
and the ends of the earth for your possession."

Psalm 2:8

✤*Hail Mary*✤

"You shall rule them with an iron rod; /
  you shall shatter them like an earthen dish."

Psalm 2:9

✤*Hail Mary*✤

And now, O kings give heed; /
  take warning, you rulers of the earth.

Psalm 2:10

✤*Hail Mary*✤

Serve the LORD with fear, and rejoice before
  him;

51

with trembling pay homage to him, /
Lest he be angry and you perish from the way,
  when his anger blazes suddenly.

Psalm 2:11-12

✤*Hail Mary*✤

Happy are all /
  who take refuge in him!

Psalm 2:12

✤*Hail Mary*✤

✤*Glory Be*✤

Second Wisdom Mystery
Passion of the Messiah

✤*Our Father*✤

My God, my God, why have you forsaken me, /
  far from my prayer, from the words of my cry?

Psalm 22:2

✤*Hail Mary*✤

But I am a worm, not a man; /
  the scorn of men, despised by the people.

Psalm 22:7

✤*Hail Mary*✤

All who see me scoff at me; /
>   they mock me with parted lips, they wag their
>   heads:

Psalm 22:8

✤*Hail Mary*✤

"He relied on the LORD; let him deliver him, /
let him rescue him, if he loves him."

Psalm 22:9

✤*Hail Mary*✤

I am like water poured out; /
>   all my bones are racked.

Psalm 22:15

✤*Hail Mary*✤

My heart has become like wax /
>   melting away within my bosom.

Psalm 22:15

✤*Hail Mary*✤

My throat is dried up like baked clay,
>   my tongue cleaves to my jaws; /
>   to the dust of death you have brought me down.

Psalm 22:16

✤*Hail Mary*✤

Indeed, many dogs surround me,

a pack of evildoers closes in upon me; /
They have pierced my hands and my feet;

Psalm 22:17

✤*Hail Mary*✤

I can count all my bones. /
They look on and gloat over me;

Psalm 22:18

✤*Hail Mary*✤

they divide my garments among them, /
and for my vesture they cast lots.

Psalm 22:19

✤*Hail Mary*✤

✤*Glory Be*✤

Third Wisdom Mystery
Victory of the Messiah

✤*Our Father*✤

I will proclaim your name to my brethren; /
in the midst of the assembly I will praise you:

Psalm 22:23

✤*Hail Mary*✤

"You who fear the LORD, praise him;
all you descendants of Jacob,
give glory to him; /

revere him, all you descendants of Israel!"
Psalm 22:24

✤*Hail Mary*✤

"For he has not spurned nor disdained
　　the wretched man in his misery, /
Nor did he turn his face away from him,
　　but when he cried out to him, he heard him."
Psalm 22:25

✤*Hail Mary*✤

So by your gift will I utter praise in the vast
　　assembly; /
　　I will fulfill my vows before those who fear him.
Psalm 22:26

✤*Hail Mary*✤

The lowly shall eat their fill; /
　　they who seek the LORD shall praise him:
　　"May your hearts be ever merry!"
Psalm 22:27

✤*Hail Mary*✤

All the ends of the earth
　　shall remember and turn to the LORD; /
All the families of the nations
　　shall bow down before him.
Psalm 22:28

55

✤Hail Mary✤

For dominion is the LORD's, /
   and he rules the nations.

Psalm 22:29

✤Hail Mary✤

To him alone shall bow down
   all who sleep in the earth; /
Before him shall bend
   all who go down into the dust.

Psalm 22:30

✤Hail Mary✤

And to him my soul shall live;
   my descendants shall serve him. /
Let the coming generation be told of the LORD.

Psalm 22:3-32

✤Hail Mary✤

that they may proclaim to a
   people yet to be born /
the justice he has shown.

Psalm 22:32

✤Hail Mary✤

✤Glory Be✤

Fourth Wisdom Mystery
The Messiah's Kingdom

✤Our Father✤

O God, with your judgment endow the king, /
   and with your justice, the king's son;

Psalm 72:1

✤Hail Mary✤

He shall govern your people with justice /
   and your afflicted ones with judgment.

Psalm 72:2

✤Hail Mary✤

May he endure as long as the sun, /
   and like the moon through all generations.

Psalm 72:5

✤Hail Mary✤

He shall be like rain coming down on the meadow, /
   like showers watering the earth.

Psalm 72:6

✤Hail Mary✤

Justice shall flower in his days, /
   and profound peace, till the moon be no more.

Psalm 72:7

✤Hail Mary✤

57

May he rule from sea to sea, /
and from the River to the ends of the earth.

Psalm 72:8

❧Hail Mary❧

The kings of Tarshish and the Isles shall offer
gifts; /
the kings of Arabia and Seba shall bring tribute.

Psalm 72:10

❧Hail Mary❧

All kings shall pay him homage, /
all nations shall serve him.

Psalm 72:11

❧Hail Mary❧

He shall have pity for the lowly and the poor; /
the lives of the poor he shall save.

Psalm 72:13

❧Hail Mary❧

May his name be blessed forever;
as long as the sun his name shall remain. /
In him shall all the tribes of the earth be blessed;
all the nations shall proclaim his happiness.

Psalm 72:17

❧Hail Mary❧

❧Glory Be❧

Fifth Wisdom Mystery
The Almighty Lord

✤*Our Father*✤

The LORD said to my Lord: "Sit at my right hand /
  till I make your enemies your footstool."

Psalm 110:1

✤*Hail Mary*✤

The scepter of your power the LORD will stretch
  forth from Zion: /
  "Rule in the midst of your enemies."

Psalm 110:2

✤*Hail Mary*✤

"Yours is princely power in the day of your birth,
  in holy splendor; /
  before the daystar, like the dew, I have
  begotten you."

Psalm 110:3

✤*Hail Mary*✤

The LORD has sworn, and he will not repent: /
  "You are a priest forever, according to the
  order of Melchizedek."

Psalm 110:4

✤*Hail Mary*✤

The stone which the builders rejected /
   has become the cornerstone.

Psalm 118:22

✣*Hail Mary*✣

Put not your trust in princes,
   in man, in whom there is no salvation. /
When his spirit departs he returns to his earth;
   on that day his plans perish.

Psalm 146:3-4

✣*Hail Mary*✣

Happy he whose help is the God of Jacob, /
   whose hope is in the LORD, his God.

Psalm 146:5

✣*Hail Mary*✣

The LORD sets captives free; /
   the LORD gives sight to the blind.

Psalm 146:7-8

✣*Hail Mary*✣

The LORD raises up those that were bowed down; /
   the LORD loves the just.

Psalm 146:8

✣*Hail Mary*✣

The L\ :sub:`ORD` shall reign forever; /
    your God, O Zion, through all generations.
    Alleluia.

Psalm 146:10

✤*Hail Mary*✤

✤*Glory Be*✤

THE EARLY-PROPHETIC MYSTERIES

Dear Jesus, through the years your Word spoke plainly of you and yet when you came the people did not see you as the savior that they had envisioned. Let me never try to make you into the savior and lord that I might think I could easily accept, but rather enlighten me and mold me into accepting you as you are — the Lord and Savior I need.

In the name of the Father, and of the Son, and of the Holy Spirit. Amen.

First Early-Prophetic Mystery
The Restoration

✤*Our Father*✤

In days to come
    the mount of the LORD's house
    Shall be established higher than the
      mountains; /
    it shall rise high above the hills,
    And peoples shall stream to it:

Micah 4:1

✤*Hail Mary*✤

Many nations shall come, and say,
"Come, let us climb the mount of the LORD,
    to the house of the God of Jacob, /
That he may instruct us in his ways,
    that we may walk in his paths."

Micah 4:2

✤*Hail Mary*✤

. . . They shall beat their swords into plowshares,
    and their spears into pruning hooks; /

63

One nation shall not raise the sword against another,
    nor shall they train for war again.

Micah 4:3

✣Hail Mary✣

For all the peoples walk
    each in the name of its god, /
But we will walk in the name of the LORD,
    our God, forever and ever.

Micah 4:5

✣Hail Mary✣

On that day, says the LORD,
    I will gather the lame, /
And I will assemble the outcasts,
    and those whom I have afflicted.

Micah 4:6

✣Hail Mary✣

I will make of the lame a remnant, /
    and of those driven far off a strong nation. . . .

Micah 4:7

✣Hail Mary✣

Now fence yourself in, Bat-gader!
    "They have laid siege against us!" /
With the rod they strike on the cheek
    the ruler of Israel.

Micah 4:14

✣Hail Mary✣

But you, Bethlehem-Ephrathah,
    too small to be among the clans of Judah, /
From you shall come forth for me
    one who is to be ruler in Israel;
Whose origin is from of old,
    from ancient times.

Micah 5:1

✤*Hail Mary*✤

He shall stand firm and shepherd his flock
    by the strength of the L ORD; . . . /
And they shall remain, for now his greatness
    shall reach to the ends of the earth.

Micah 5:3

✤*Hail Mary*✤

The remnant of Jacob shall be
    in the midst of many peoples, /
Like dew coming from the L ORD,
    like raindrops on the grass. . . .

Micah 5:6

✤*Hail Mary*✤

✤*Glory Be*✤

Second Early-Prophetic Mystery
The Birth of Immanuel

✤*Our Father*✤

"Therefore the LORD himself will give you this
    sign: /
the virgin shall be with child, and bear a son, and
    shall name him Immanuel."

Isaiah 7:14

✤*Hail Mary*✤

Yet he shall be a snare, an obstacle and a
    stumbling stone
    to both the houses of Israel, /
A trap and a snare
    to those who dwell in Jerusalem;

Isaiah 8:14

✤*Hail Mary*✤

And many among them shall stumble and fall, /
    broken, snared, and captured.

Isaiah 8:15

✤*Hail Mary*✤

The people who walked in darkness
    have seen a great light; /
Upon those who dwelt in the land of gloom
    a light has shone.

Isaiah 9:1

✤*Hail Mary*✤

You have brought them abundant joy
    and great rejoicing, /
As they rejoice before you as at the harvest,
    as men make merry when dividing spoils.

Isaiah 9:2

✤*Hail Mary*✤

For the yoke that burdened them,
    the pole on their shoulder,
And the rod of their taskmaster /
    you have smashed, as on the day of Midian.

Isaiah 9:3

✤*Hail Mary*✤

For a child is born to us, a son is given us; /
    upon his shoulder dominion rests.

Isaiah 9:5

✤*Hail Mary*✤

They name him Wonder-Counselor, God-Hero, /
    Father-Forever, Prince of Peace.

Isaiah 9:5

✤*Hail Mary*✤

His dominion is vast
    and forever peaceful, /
From David's throne, and over his kingdom,
    which he confirms and sustains. . . .

Isaiah 9:6

✤*Hail Mary*✤

By judgment and justice,
    both now and forever. /
The zeal of the LORD of hosts will do this!

Isaiah 9:6

✤*Hail Mary*✤

✤*Glory Be*✤

Third Early-Prophetic Mystery
The Reign of Immanuel

✤*Our Father*✤

But a shoot shall sprout from the stump of Jesse, /
    and from his roots a bud shall blossom.

Isaiah 11:1

✤*Hail Mary*✤

The spirit of the LORD shall rest upon him: . . . /
    and his delight shall be the fear of the Lord.

Isaiah 11:2-3

✤*Hail Mary*✤

Not by appearance shall he judge,
    nor by hearsay shall he decide, /

But he shall judge the poor with justice,
and decide aright for the land's afflicted.

Isaiah 11:3-4

✤*Hail Mary*✤

He shall strike the ruthless with the rod of his
mouth, /
and with the breath of his lips he shall slay
the wicked.

Isaiah 11:4

✤*Hail Mary*✤

Justice shall be the band around his waist, /
and faithfulness a belt upon his hips.

Isaiah 11:5

✤*Hail Mary*✤

Then the wolf shall be a guest of the lamb,
and the leopard shall lie down with the kid; /
The calf and the young lion shall browse together,
with a little child to guide them.

Isaiah 11:6

✤*Hail Mary*✤

There shall be no harm or ruin on all my holy
mountain; /

69

for the earth shall be filled with knowledge of
   the LORD,
      as water covers the sea.

Isaiah 11:9

✤*Hail Mary*✤

On that day,
The root of Jesse,
   set up as a signal for the nations, /
The Gentiles shall seek out,
   for his dwelling shall be glorious.

Isaiah 11:10

✤*Hail Mary*✤

He shall raise a signal to the nations
   and gather the outcasts of Israel; /
The dispersed of Judah he shall assemble
   from the four corners of the earth.

Isaiah 11:12

✤*Hail Mary*✤

and say on that day:
Give thanks to the LORD, acclaim his name; /
   among the nations make known his deeds,
   proclaim how exalted is his name.

Isaiah 12:4

✤*Hail Mary*✤

✤*Glory Be*✤

Fourth Early-Prophetic Mystery
The Deliverer

✤*Our Father*✤

Indeed the LORD will be there with us, majestic; /
yes, the LORD our judge, the LORD our lawgiver,
the LORD our king, he it is who will save us.

Isaiah 33:22

✤*Hail Mary*✤

No one who dwells there will say, "I am sick"; /
the people who live there will be forgiven
their guilt.

Isaiah 33:24

✤*Hail Mary*✤

The desert and the parched land will exult . . . /
They will see the glory of the LORD,
the splendor of our God.

Isaiah 35:1-2

✤*Hail Mary*✤

Then will the eyes of the blind be opened, /
the ears of the deaf be cleared;

Isaiah 35:5

✤*Hail Mary*✤

Then will the lame leap like a stag, /

71

then the tongue of the dumb will sing.

Isaiah 35:6

✣Hail Mary✣

A highway will be there,
  called the holy way; /
No one unclean may pass over it,
  nor fools go astray on it.

Isaiah 35:8

✣Hail Mary✣

Those whom the LORD has ransomed will return
  and enter Zion singing,
  crowned with everlasting joy; /
They will meet with joy and gladness,
  sorrow and mourning will flee.

Isaiah 35:10

✣Hail Mary✣

Here is my servant whom I uphold,
  my chosen one with whom I am pleased, /
Upon whom I have put my spirit;
  he shall bring forth justice to the nations,

Isaiah 42:1

✣Hail Mary✣

A bruised reed he shall not break,
  and a smoldering wick he shall not quench, /

72

Until he establishes justice on the earth;
the coastlands will wait for his teaching.

Isaiah 42:3-4

✤*Hail Mary*✤

See, the earlier things have come to pass,
new ones I now foretell; /
Before they spring into being,
I announce them to you.

Isaiah 42:9

✤*Hail Mary*✤

✤*Glory Be*✤

Fifth Early-Prophetic Mystery **The Suffering Servant**

✤*Our Father*✤

He grew up like a sapling before him,
like a shoot from the parched earth; /
There was in him no stately bearing to make us
look at him,
nor appearance that would attract us to him.

Isaiah 53:2

✤*Hail Mary*✤

He was spurned and avoided by men,

a man of suffering, accustomed to infirmity, /
One of those from whom men hide their faces,
    spurned, and we held him in no esteem.

Isaiah 53:3

✤Hail Mary✤

Yet it was our infirmities that he bore,
    our sufferings that he endured, /
While we thought of him as stricken,
    as one smitten by God and afflicted.

Isaiah 53:4

✤Hail Mary✤

But he was pierced for our offenses,
    crushed for our sins, /
Upon him was the chastisement that makes us
    whole,
    by his stripes we were healed.

Isaiah 53:5

✤Hail Mary✤

We had all gone astray like sheep,
    each following his own way; /
But the LORD laid upon him
    the guilt of us all.

Isaiah 53:6

✤Hail Mary✤

Though he was harshly treated, he submitted

and opened not his mouth; /
Like a lamb led to the slaughter
   or a sheep before the shearers,
   he was silent and opened not his mouth.

Isaiah 53:7

✤*Hail Mary*✤

Oppressed and condemned, he was taken away,
   and who would have thought any more of his
   destiny? /
When he was cut off from the land of the living,
   and smitten for the sins of his people,

Isaiah 53:8

✤*Hail Mary*✤

A grave was assigned him among the wicked
   and a burial place with evildoers, /
Though he had done no wrong
   nor spoken any falsehood.

Isaiah 53:9

✤*Hail Mary*✤

Because of his affliction
   he shall see the light in fullness of days; /
Through his suffering, my servant shall justify
   many,
     and their guilt he shall bear.

Isaiah 53:11

♣*Hail Mary*♣

Therefore I will give him his portion among the
    great,
    and he shall divide the spoils with the mighty, /
Because he surrendered himself to death
    and was counted among the wicked;
And he shall take away the sins of many,
    and win pardon for their offenses.

Isaiah 53:12

♣*Hail Mary*♣

♣*Glory Be*♣

THE LATE-PROPHETIC MYSTERIES

In the fullness of time, Lord, you prepared your people for a new covenant in which all who would follow you could truly know you. Let me know that great expectation and joy that was experienced by your faithful as they awaited the

77

arrival of the glorious Day of the Lord. Help me
to now follow and experience you in the fullness
which you desire.

In the name of the Father, and of the Son, and
of the Holy Spirit. Amen.

First Late-Prophetic Mystery
The New Covenant

✤*Our Father*✤

Behold, the days are coming, says the LORD, /
   when I will raise up a righteous shoot to
   David;

Jeremiah 23:5

✤*Hail Mary*✤

As king he shall reign and govern wisely, /
   he shall do what is just and right in the land.

Jeremiah 23:5

✤*Hail Mary*✤

In his days Judah shall be saved, /
   Israel shall dwell in security.

Jeremiah 23:6

✤*Hail Mary*✤

This is the name they give him: /

"The LORD our justice."

Jeremiah 23:6

✤*Hail Mary*✤

Thus says the LORD: In Ramah is heard the sound
   of moaning,
      of bitter weeping! /
Rachel mourns her children,
      she refuses to be consoled
      because her children are no more.

Jeremiah 31:15

✤*Hail Mary*✤

The days are coming, says the LORD, /
when I will make a new covenant with the house
   of Israel and the house of Judah.

Jeremiah 31:31

✤*Hail Mary*✤

It will not be like the covenant I made with their
      fathers the day I took them by the hand to
      lead them forth from the land of Egypt; /
for they broke my covenant and I had to show
      myself their master, says the LORD.

Jeremiah 31:32

✤*Hail Mary*✤

But this is the covenant which I will make with
      the house of Israel after those days, says the
      LORD. /

79

I will place my law within them, and write it
upon their hearts; I will be their God, and
they shall be my people.

Jeremiah 31:33

✤*Hail Mary*✤

No longer will they have need to teach their
friends and kinsmen how to know the LORD. /
All, from the least to greatest, shall know me,
says the Lord,

Jeremiah 31:34

✤*Hail Mary*✤

for I will forgive their evildoing /
and remember their sin no more.

Jeremiah 31:34

✤*Hail Mary*✤

✤*Glory Be*✤

Second Late-Prophetic Mystery
Day of the Lord

✤*Our Father*✤

Blow the trumpet in Zion,
sound the alarm on my holy mountain! /

Let all who dwell in the land tremble,
    for the day of the Lᴏʀᴅ is coming;

Joel 2:1

✠*Hail Mary*✠

Yet even now, says the Lᴏʀᴅ, /
    return to me with your whole heart,
        with fasting, and weeping, and mourning;

Joel 2:12

✠*Hail Mary*✠

Rend your hearts, not your garments,
    and return to the Lᴏʀᴅ, your God. /
For gracious and merciful is he,
    slow to anger, rich in kindness,
    and relenting in punishment.

Joel 2:13

✠*Hail Mary*✠

And do you, O children of Zion, exult
    and rejoice in the Lᴏʀᴅ, your God! /
He has given you the teacher of justice . . .

Joel 2:23

✠*Hail Mary*✠

You shall eat and be filled,
    and shall praise the name of the Lᴏʀᴅ, your God, /
Because he has dealt wondrously with you. . . .

Joel 2:26

✣Hail Mary✣

And you shall know that I am in the midst of
    Israel; /
I am the LORD, your God, and there is no other. . . .
Joel 2:27

✣Hail Mary✣

Then afterward I will pour out
    my spirit / upon all mankind.
Joel 3:1

✣Hail Mary✣

Your sons and daughters shall prophesy, /
    your old men shall dream dreams,
    your young men shall see visions;
Joel 3:1

✣Hail Mary✣

Even upon the servants and the handmaids, /
    in those days, I will pour out my spirit.
Joel 3:2

✣Hail Mary✣

Then everyone shall be rescued /
    who calls on the name of the LORD. . . .
Joel 3:5

✣Hail Mary✣

✣Glory Be✣

Third Late-Prophetic Mystery
The King of Israel

✤*Our Father*✤

Silence in the presence of the Lord God!
  for near is the day of the Lord, /
Yes, the Lord has prepared a slaughter feast,
  he has consecrated his guests.

Zephaniah 1:7

✤*Hail Mary*✤

For then I will change and purify
  the lips of the peoples, /
That they all may call upon the name of the Lord,
  to serve him with one accord;

Zephaniah 3:9

✤*Hail Mary*✤

But I will leave as a remnant in your midst
  a people humble and lowly, /
Who shall take refuge in the name of the Lord;

Zephaniah 3:12

✤*Hail Mary*✤

Shout for joy, O daughter Zion!
  sing joyfully, O Israel! /
Be glad and exult with all your heart,

O daughter Jerusalem!

Zephaniah 3:14

✤*Hail Mary*✤

The LORD has removed the judgment against you, /
he has turned away your enemies;

Zephaniah 3:15

✤*Hail Mary*✤

The King of Israel, the LORD, is in your midst, /
you have no further misfortune to fear.

Zephaniah 3:15

✤*Hail Mary*✤

The LORD, your God, is in your midst, /
a mighty savior;

Zephaniah 3:17

✤*Hail Mary*✤

He will rejoice over you with gladness,
and renew you in his love, /
He will sing joyfully because of you,
as one sings at festivals.

Zephaniah 3:17-18

✤*Hail Mary*✤

Yes, at that time I will deal
with all who oppress you: /

84

I will save the lame,
    and assemble the outcasts. . . .

Zephaniah 3:19

✤*Hail Mary*✤

At that time I will bring you home,
    and at that time I will gather you; /
For I will give you renown and praise,
    among all the peoples of the earth. . . .

Zephaniah 3:20

✤*Hail Mary*✤

✤*Glory Be*✤

Fourth Late-Prophetic Mystery
The Coming of the Lord

✤*Our Father*✤

Sing and rejoice, O daughter Zion! /
See, I am coming to dwell among you, says the
LORD.

Zechariah 2:14

✤*Hail Mary*✤

Many nations shall join themselves to the LORD
    on that day, and they shall be his people, /

and he will dwell among you, and you shall
   know that the LORD of hosts has sent me to
   you.

Zechariah 2:15

❖Hail Mary❖

Silence, all mankind, in the presence of the LORD! /
for he stirs forth from his holy dwelling.

Zechariah 2:17

❖Hail Mary❖

Listen. . . Yes, I will bring my servant the
   Shoot . . . /
and I will take away the guilt of the land in one
   day.

Zechariah 3:8-9

❖Hail Mary❖

Rejoice heartily, O daughter Zion,
   shout for joy, O daughter Jerusalem!
See, your king shall come to you;
   a just savior is he, /
Meek, and riding on an ass,
   on a colt, the foal of an ass.

Zechariah 9:9

❖Hail Mary❖

. . . His dominion shall be from sea to sea, /
   and from the River to the ends of the earth.

Zechariah 9:10

✤*Hail Mary*✤

As for you, for the blood of your covenant with
    me, /
I will bring forth your prisoners from the dungeon.
Zechariah 9:11

✤*Hail Mary*✤

In the return to the fortress
    of the waiting prisoners, /
This very day, I will return you
    double for your exile.
Zechariah 9:12

✤*Hail Mary*✤

The LORD of hosts shall be a shield over them . . .
    and trample them underfoot; /
They shall drink blood like wine,
    till they are filled with it like libation bowls,
    like the corners of the altar.
Zechariah 9:15

✤*Hail Mary*✤

And the LORD, their God, shall save them on that
    day,
    his people, like a flock. /
For they are the jewels in a crown
    raised aloft over his land.
Zechariah 9:16

✤*Hail Mary*✤

✤*Glory Be*✤

Fifth Late-Prophetic Mystery
Messenger of the Covenant

✤*Our Father*✤

Lo, I am sending my messenger /
  to prepare the way before me;

Malachi 3:1

✤*Hail Mary*✤

And suddenly there will come to the temple
  the LORD whom you seek, /
And the messenger of the covenant whom you
  desire. . . .

Malachi 3:1

✤*Hail Mary*✤

But who will endure the day of his coming? /
  And who can stand when he appears?

Malachi 3:2

✤*Hail Mary*✤

For he is like the refiner's fire,
  or like the fuller's lye. /
He will sit refining and purifying. . . .

Malachi 3:2-3

✤*Hail Mary*✤

and he will purify the sons of Levi, /
Refining them like gold or like silver
    that they may offer due sacrifice to the Lord.

Malachi 3:3

✤*Hail Mary*✤

Then the sacrifice of Judah and Jerusalem
    will please the LORD, /
    as in the days of old, as in years gone by.

Malachi 3:4

✤*Hail Mary*✤

Then you will again see the distinction
    between the just and the wicked; /
Between him who serves God,
    and him who does not serve him.

Malachi 3:18

✤*Hail Mary*✤

For lo, the day is coming, blazing like an oven,
    when all the proud and all evildoers will be
    stubble, /
And the day that is coming will set them on fire,
    leaving them neither root nor branch,
    says the LORD of hosts.

Malachi 3:19

✤*Hail Mary*✤

But for you who fear my name, there will arise
    the sun of justice with its healing rays; /
And you will gambol like calves out of the stall.

Malachi 3:20

✤Hail Mary✤

Lo, I will send you
    Elijah, the prophet, /
Before the day of the Lord comes,
    the great and terrible day.

Malachi 3:23

✤Hail Mary✤

✤Glory Be✤

THE ANNUNCIATION MYSTERIES

Dear Lord, help me to put such trust in you that the impossible can become possible in my life as it did with Elizabeth and Zechariah. Strengthen me to be pure and faithful, after the example of the Holy Virgin, Mary, that the unbelievably wondrous plan of God might be fostered in the world by my actions.

In the name of the Father, and of the Son, and of the Holy Spirit. Amen.

First Annunciation Mystery
Announcement of the Birth of John

✠*Our Father*✠

In the days of Herod, King of Judea, there was a priest named Zechariah of the priestly division of Abijah; /
his wife was from the daughters of Aaron, and her name was Elizabeth.

Luke 1:5

✠*Hail Mary*✠

Both were righteous in the eyes of God, /
observing all the commandments and ordinances of the Lord blamelessly.

Luke 1:6

✠*Hail Mary*✠

But they had no child, because Elizabeth was barren /
and both were advanced in years.

Luke 1:7

✤*Hail Mary*✤

Once when he was serving as priest in his
    division's turn before God . . . /
the angel of the Lord appeared to him, standing
    at the right of the altar of incense.

Luke 1:8, 11

✤*Hail Mary*✤

Zechariah was troubled by what he saw, /
and fear came upon him.

Luke 1:12

✤*Hail Mary*✤

But the angel said to him, "Do not be afraid,
    Zechariah, because your prayer has been
    heard. /
Your wife Elizabeth will bear you a son, and you
    shall name him John.

Luke 1:13

✤*Hail Mary*✤

And you will have joy and gladness, /
and many will rejoice at his birth,

Luke 1:14

✤*Hail Mary*✤

for he will be great in the sight of [the] Lord. He

will drink neither wine nor strong drink. /
He will be filled with the holy Spirit even from
his mother's womb,

Luke 1:15

✤*Hail Mary*✤

and he will turn many of the children of Israel /
to the Lord their God.

Luke 1:16

✤*Hail Mary*✤

He will go before him in the spirit and power of
Elijah to turn the hearts of fathers toward
children /
and the disobedient to understanding of the
righteous, to prepare a people fit for the Lord.

Luke 1:17

✤*Hail Mary*✤

✤*Glory Be*✤

Second Annunciation Mystery
Announcement of the Birth of Jesus

✤*Our Father*✤

In the sixth month, the angel Gabriel was sent

from God /
to a town of Galilee called Nazareth;

Luke 1:26

♣*Hail Mary*♣

to a virgin betrothed to a man named Joseph, of
the house of David, /
and the virgin's name was Mary.

Luke 1:27

♣*Hail Mary*♣

And coming to her, he said, /
"Hail favored one! The Lord is with you."

Luke 1:28

♣*Hail Mary*♣

But she was greatly troubled at what was said /
and pondered what sort of greeting this might be.

Luke 1:29

♣*Hail Mary*♣

Then the angel said to her, "Do not be afraid,
Mary, /
for you have found favor with God."

Luke 1:30

♣*Hail Mary*♣

"Behold, you will conceive in your womb and

bear a son, /
and you shall name him Jesus."

Luke 1:31

✠*Hail Mary*✠

"He will be great and will be called Son of the
Most High, /
and the Lord God will give him the throne of
David his father,"

Luke 1:32

✠*Hail Mary*✠

"and he will rule over the house of Jacob forever, /
and of his kingdom there will be no end."

Luke 1:33

✠*Hail Mary*✠

But Mary said to the angel, "How can this be,
since I have no relations with a man?" /
And the angel said to her in reply, "The holy
Spirit will come upon you, and the power of
the Most High will overshadow you."

Luke 1:34-35

✠*Hail Mary*✠

"Therefore the child to be born will be called holy, /
the Son of God."

Luke 1:35

✤*Hail Mary*✤

✤*Glory Be*✤

Third Annunciation Mystery
Mary Visits Elizabeth

✤*Our Father*✤

"And behold, Elizabeth, your relative, has also
conceived a son in her old age, /
and this is the sixth month for her who was called
barren;"

Luke 1:36

✤*Hail Mary*✤

"for nothing will be impossible /
for God."

Luke 1:37

✤*Hail Mary*✤

Mary said, "Behold, I am the handmaid of the
Lord. May it be done to me according to
your word." /
Then the angel departed from her.

Luke 1:38

✤*Hail Mary*✤

During those days Mary set out and traveled to

97

the hill country in haste /
to a town of Judah,

Luke 1:39

✤Hail Mary✤

where she entered the house of Zechariah /
and greeted Elizabeth.

Luke 1:40

✤Hail Mary✤

When Elizabeth heard Mary's greeting, /
the infant leaped in her womb, . . .

Luke 1:41

✤Hail Mary✤

Elizabeth, filled with the holy Spirit, cried out in
a loud voice and said, /
"Most blessed are you among women, and
blessed is the fruit of your womb."

Luke 1:41-42

✤Hail Mary✤

"And how does this happen to me, /
that the mother of my Lord should come to me?"

Luke 1:43

✤Hail Mary✤

"For at the moment the sound of your greeting
reached my ears, /

98

the infant in my womb leaped for joy."

Luke 1:44

✤*Hail Mary*✤

"Blessed are you who believed /
that what was spoken to you by the Lord would
    be fulfilled."

Luke 1:45

✤*Hail Mary*✤

✤*Glory Be*✤

Fourth Annunciation Mystery
The Canticle of Mary

✤*Our Father*✤

And Mary said: /
"My soul proclaims the greatness of the Lord;"

Luke 1:46

✤*Hail Mary*✤

"my spirit rejoices /
in God my savior."

Luke 1:47

✤*Hail Mary*✤

"For he has looked upon his handmaid's
    lowliness; /

99

behold, from now on will all ages call me
blessed."

Luke 1:48

✤*Hail Mary*✤

"The Mighty One has done great things for me, /
and holy is his name."

Luke 1:49

✤*Hail Mary*✤

"His mercy is from age to age /
to those who fear him."

Luke 1:50

✤*Hail Mary*✤

"He has shown might with his arm, /
dispersed the arrogant of mind and heart."

Luke 1:51

✤*Hail Mary*✤

"He has thrown down the rulers from their
thrones /
but lifted up the lowly."

Luke 1:52

✤*Hail Mary*✤

"The hungry he has filled with good things; /
the rich he has sent away empty."

Luke 1:53

✤*Hail Mary*✤

"He has helped Israel his servant,
   remembering his mercy, /
according to his promise to our fathers,
   to Abraham and to his descendants forever."

Luke 1:54-55

✤*Hail Mary*✤

Mary remained with her about three months /
and then returned to her home.

Luke 1:56

✤*Hail Mary*✤

✤*Glory Be*✤

Fifth Annunciation Mystery
The Birth of John

✤*Our Father*✤

When the time arrived for Elizabeth to have her
   child /
she gave birth to a son.

Luke 1:57

✤*Hail Mary*✤

Her neighbors and relatives heard that the Lord
   had shown his great mercy toward her, /

101

and they rejoiced with her.

Luke 1:58

✤Hail Mary✤

. . . saying, "What then, will this child be?" /
For surely the hand of the Lord was with him.

Luke 1:66

✤Hail Mary✤

Then Zechariah his father, filled with the holy
      Spirit, prophesied, saying: /
"Blessed be the Lord, the God of Israel,
    for he has visited and brought redemption to
      his people."

Luke 1:67-68

✤Hail Mary✤

"He has raised up a horn for our salvation
    within the house of David his servant, /
even as he promised through the mouth of his
    holy prophets from of old:"

Luke 1:69-70

✤Hail Mary✤

". . . to be mindful of his holy covenant /
and of the oath he swore to Abraham our father,"

Luke 1:72-73

✤Hail Mary✤

"And you, child, will be called prophet of the
    Most High, /
    for you will go before the Lord to prepare his
    ways,"

Luke 1:76

✤Hail Mary✤

"to give his people knowledge of salvation /
    through the forgiveness of their sins,"

Luke 1:77

✤Hail Mary✤

"to shine on those who sit in darkness and
    death's shadow, /
    to guide our feet into the path of peace."

Luke 1:79

✤Hail Mary✤

The child grew and became strong in spirit, /
and he was in the desert until the day of his
    manifestation to Israel.

Luke 1:80

✤Hail Mary✤

✤Glory Be✤

THE NATIVITY MYSTERIES

O my God, what great love you have shown me in that you have sent your very best for me, your Son. Who could have imagined that the world's Creator would himself come as the Savior? Help me to be filled with awe and wonder at your coming, as were the shepherds

and the magi. Let me follow the example of our
dear mother, Mary, in loving you.

In the name of the Father, and of the Son, and
of the Holy Spirit. Amen.

First Nativity Mystery
The Word Becomes Flesh

✤*Our Father*✤

In the beginning was the Word, /
   and the Word was with God,
   and the Word was God.

John 1:1

✤*Hail Mary*✤

He was in the beginning with God. /
All things came to be through him,
   and without him nothing came to be.

John 1:2-3

✤*Hail Mary*✤

What came to be through him was life, /
   and this life was the light of the human race;

John 1:3-4

✤*Hail Mary*✤

the light shines in the darkness, /
   and the darkness has not overcome it.

John 1:5

✤Hail Mary✤

A man named John was sent from God. /
He came for testimony, to testify to the light, so
    that all might believe through him.

John 1:6-7

✤Hail Mary✤

He was not the light, /
but came to testify to the light.

John 1:8

✤Hail Mary✤

The true light, which enlightens everyone, /
was coming into the world.

John 1:9

✤Hail Mary✤

He was in the world, and the world came to be
    through him, /
    but the world did not know him.

John 1:10

✤Hail Mary✤

He came to what was his own,
    but his own people did not accept him. /
But to those who did accept him he gave power
    to become children of God. . . .

John 1:11-12

✤*Hail Mary*✤

And the Word became flesh
   and made his dwelling among us, /
   and we saw his glory,
   the glory as of the Father's only Son,
   full of grace and truth.

John 1:14

✤*Hail Mary*✤

✤*Glory Be*✤

Second Nativity Mystery
Preparation for the Birth of Christ

✤*Our Father*✤

Now this is how the birth /
of Jesus Christ came about.

Matthew 1:18

✤*Hail Mary*✤

When his mother Mary was betrothed to Joseph,
   but before they lived together, /
she was found with child through the holy Spirit.

Matthew 1:18

✤*Hail Mary*✤

Joseph her husband, since he was a righteous
     man, yet unwilling to expose her to shame, /
decided to divorce her quietly.

Matthew 1:19

✤Hail Mary✤

Such was his intention when, behold, /
the angel of the Lord appeared to him in a
     dream . . .

Matthew 1:20

✤Hail Mary✤

and said, "Joseph, son of David, do not be afraid
     to take Mary your wife into your home. /
For it is through the holy Spirit that this child has
     been conceived in her."

Matthew 1:20

✤Hail Mary✤

"She will bear a son and you are to name him
     Jesus, /
because he will save his people from their sins."

Matthew 1:21

✤Hail Mary✤

All this took place to fulfill /
what the Lord had said through the prophet:

Matthew 1:22

✤Hail Mary✤

"Behold, the virgin shall be with child and bear
    a son, /
and they shall name him Emmanuel,"
which means "God is with us."

Matthew 1:23

✤*Hail Mary*✤

When Joseph awoke, he did as the angel of the
    Lord had commanded him /
and took his wife into his home.

Matthew 1:24

✤*Hail Mary*✤

He had no relations with her until she bore a son, /
and he named him Jesus.

Matthew 1:25

✤*Hail Mary*✤

✤*Glory Be*✤

Third Nativity Mystery
The Birth of Jesus

✤*Our Father*✤

In those days a decree went out from Caesar
    Augustus that the whole world should be
    enrolled. . . . /

109

So all went to be enrolled, each to his own town.

Luke 2:1-3

✤*Hail Mary*✤

And Joseph too went up from Galilee . . . to the city of David that is called Bethlehem . . . / to be enrolled with Mary, his betrothed, who was with child.

Luke 2:4-5

✤*Hail Mary*✤

While they were there, the time came for her to have her child, / and she gave birth to her firstborn son.

Luke 2:6-7

✤*Hail Mary*✤

She wrapped him in swaddling clothes and laid him in a manger, / because there was no room for them in the inn.

Luke 2:7

✤*Hail Mary*✤

Now there were shepherds in that region living in the fields and keeping the night watch over their flock. / The angel of the Lord appeared to them and the glory of the Lord shone around them, and they were struck with great fear.

Luke 2:8-9

✤*Hail Mary*✤

The angel said to them, "Do not be afraid; for behold, /
I proclaim to you good news of great joy that will be for all the people."

Luke 2:10

✤*Hail Mary*✤

"For today in the city of David a savior has been born for you /
who is Messiah and Lord."

Luke 2:11

✤*Hail Mary*✤

"And this will be a sign for you: /
You will find an infant wrapped in swaddling clothes and lying in a manger."

Luke 2:12

✤*Hail Mary*✤

And suddenly there was a multitude of the heavenly host with the angel, /
praising God and saying:

Luke 2:13

✤*Hail Mary*✤

"Glory to God in the highest /
and on earth peace to those
   on whom his favor rests."

Luke 2:14

❧Hail Mary❧

❧Glory Be❧

Fourth Nativity Mystery
Visitation of the Shepherds

❧Our Father❧

. . . "Holy, holy, holy is the Lord God almighty, /
who was, and who is, and who is to come."

Revelation 4:8

❧Hail Mary❧

. . . "Salvation comes from our God, who is
   seated on the throne, /
and from the Lamb."

Revelation 7:10

❧Hail Mary❧

. . . "Amen. Blessing and glory, wisdom and
   thanksgiving, /
honor, power, and might
be to our God forever and ever. Amen."

Revelation 7:12

✤Hail Mary✤

When the angels went away from them to
    heaven, the shepherds said to one another, /
"Let us go, then, to Bethlehem to see this thing
    that has taken place, which the Lord has
    made known to us."

Luke 2:15

✤Hail Mary✤

So they went in haste /
and found Mary and Joseph, and the infant lying
    in the manger.

Luke 2:16

✤Hail Mary✤

When they saw this, they made known the
    message /
that had been told them about this child.

Luke 2:17

✤Hail Mary✤

All who heard it were amazed /
by what had been told them by the shepherds.

Luke 2:18

✤Hail Mary✤

And Mary kept all these things, /
reflecting on them in her heart.

Luke 2:19

✤*Hail Mary*✤

Then the shepherds returned, glorifying and
praising God for all they had heard and seen, /
just as it had been told to them.

Luke 2:20

✤*Hail Mary*✤

When eight days were completed for his
circumcision, he was named Jesus, /
the name given him by the angel before he was
conceived in the womb.

Luke 2:21

✤*Hail Mary*✤

✤*Glory Be*✤

Fifth Nativity Mystery
Coming of the Magi

✤*Our Father*✤

. . . behold, magi from the east arrived in
Jerusalem, saying, "Where is the newborn
king of the Jews? /
We saw his star at its rising and have come to do
him homage."

Matthew 2:1-2

✤*Hail Mary*✤

114

When King Herod heard this, he was greatly
   troubled, /
and all Jerusalem with him.

Matthew 2:3

✠*Hail Mary*✠

Assembling all the chief priests and the scribes
   of the people, /
he inquired of them where the Messiah was to be born.

Matthew 2:4

✠*Hail Mary*✠

They said to him, "In Bethlehem of Judea, for
   thus it has been written through the prophet: /
'. . . from you shall come a ruler,
   who is to shepherd my people Israel.' "

Matthew 2:5-6

✠*Hail Mary*✠

Then Herod called the magi secretly /
and ascertained from them the time of the star's
   appearance.

Matthew 2:7

✠*Hail Mary*✠

He sent them to Bethlehem and said, "Go and
   search diligently for the child. /

115

When you have found him, bring me word, that I too may go and do him homage."

Matthew 2:8

✤*Hail Mary*✤

After their audience with the king they set out.
    And behold, the star that they had seen at its
    rising preceded them, /
until it came and stopped over the place where
    the child was.

Matthew 2:9

✤*Hail Mary*✤

They were overjoyed at seeing the star, /
and on entering the house they saw the child
    with Mary his mother.

Matthew 2:10-11

✤*Hail Mary*✤

They prostrated themselves and did him
    homage. /
Then they opened their treasures and offered him
    gifts of gold, frankincense, and myrrh.

Matthew 2:11

✤*Hail Mary*✤

And having been warned in a dream not to
    return to Herod, /
they departed for their country by another way.

Matthew 2:12

✤*Hail Mary*✤

✤*Glory Be*✤

THE PAROUSIA
MYSTERIES

*D*ear *Jesus, help me to always be ready to meet you face to face, whether it be upon the day of your return or at the hour of my death. Lord, please mold me to be like Noah, who was prepared, so that I may one day dwell within the*

fullness of your new Jerusalem — your bride — and
experience your glorious presence forever.

  In the name of the Father, and of the Son, and
of the Holy Spirit. Amen.

First Parousia Mystery
The Sign of Christ's Coming

✤*Our Father*✤

As he was sitting on the Mount of Olives, the
  disciples approached him privately and said, /
"Tell us, when will this happen, and what sign
  will there be of your coming, and of the end
  of the age?"

Matthew 24:3

✤*Hail Mary*✤

Jesus said to them in reply, "See that no one
  deceives you. /
For many will come in my name, saying, 'I am
  the Messiah,' and they will deceive many."

Matthew 24:4-5

✤*Hail Mary*✤

"You will hear of wars and reports of wars; see
  that you are not alarmed, /
for these things must happen, but it will not yet
  be the end."

Matthew 24:6

119

✤Hail Mary✤

"Nation will rise against nation, and kingdom
   against kingdom; there will be famines and
   earthquakes from place to place. /
All these are the beginnings of the labor pains."

Matthew 24:7-8

✤Hail Mary✤

"Then they will hand you over to persecution,
   and they will kill you. You will be hated by
   all nations because of my name. /
And then many will be led into sin; they will
   betray and hate one another."

Matthew 24:9-10

✤Hail Mary✤

"Many false prophets will arise and deceive many; /
and because of the increase of evildoing, the
   love of many will grow cold."

Matthew 24:11-12

✤Hail Mary✤

"But the one who perseveres to the end /
will be saved."

Matthew 24:13

✤Hail Mary✤

"And this gospel of the kingdom will be

preached throughout the world as a witness
to all nations, /
and then the end will come."

Matthew 24:14

✤*Hail Mary*✤

"And then the sign of the Son of Man will appear
in heaven, and all the tribes of the earth will
mourn, /
and they will see the Son of Man coming upon
the clouds of heaven with power and great
glory."

Matthew 24:30

✤*Hail Mary*✤

"And he will send out his angels with a trumpet
blast, /
and they will gather his elect from the four winds,
from one end of the heavens to the other."

Matthew 24:31

✤*Hail Mary*✤

✤*Glory Be*✤

Second Parousia Mystery
The Unknown Day

✣*Our Father*✣

"In the same way, when you see all these things, /
know that he is near, at the gates."

Matthew 24:33

✣*Hail Mary*✣

"But of that day and hour no one knows, /
neither the angels of heaven, nor the Son, but the
Father alone."

Matthew 24:36

✣*Hail Mary*✣

"For as it was in the days of Noah, /
so it will be at the coming of the Son of Man."

Matthew 24:37

✣*Hail Mary*✣

"In [those] days before the flood, they were
eating and drinking, marrying and giving in
marriage, /
up to the day that Noah entered the ark."

Matthew 24:38

✣*Hail Mary*✣

"They did not know until the flood came and
carried them all away. /

122

So will it be [also] at the coming of the Son of Man."

Matthew 24:39

❧Hail Mary❧

"Two men will be out in the field; /
one will be taken, and one will be left."

Matthew 24:40

❧Hail Mary❧

"Two women will be grinding at the mill; /
one will be taken, and one will be left."

Matthew 24:41

❧Hail Mary❧

"Therefore, stay awake! /
For you do not know on which day your Lord
will come."

Matthew 24:42

❧Hail Mary❧

"Be sure of this: if the master of the house had
known the hour of night when the thief was
coming, /
he would have stayed awake and not let his
house be broken into."

Matthew 24:43

❧Hail Mary❧

"So too, you also must be prepared, /

for at an hour you do not expect, the Son of Man
will come."

Matthew 24:44

✤*Hail Mary*✤

✤*Glory Be*✤

Third Parousia Mystery
Christ's Coming in Power

✤*Our Father*✤

Know this first of all, that in the last days scoffers
will come. . . . /
saying, "Where is the promise of his coming?"

2 Peter 3:3-4

✤*Hail Mary*✤

But do not ignore this one fact, beloved, that with
the Lord /
one day is like a thousand years and a thousand
years like one day.

2 Peter 3:8

✤*Hail Mary*✤

The Lord does not delay his promise, as some
regard "delay," /
but he is patient with you, not wishing that any

124

should perish but that all should come to repentance.

2 Peter 3:9

✤*Hail Mary*✤

But the day of the Lord will come like a thief, and then the heavens will pass away with a mighty roar /
and the elements will be dissolved by fire, and the earth and everything done on it will be found out.

2 Peter 3:10

✤*Hail Mary*✤

But according to his promise we await new heavens /
and a new earth in which righteousness dwells.

2 Peter 3:13

✤*Hail Mary*✤

For the Lord himself, with a word of command, with the voice of an archangel and with the trumpet of God, /
will come down from heaven, and the dead in Christ will rise first.

1 Thessalonians 4:16

✤*Hail Mary*✤

Then we who are alive, who are left, will be
caught up /
together with them in the clouds to meet the Lord
in the air. . . .

1 Thessalonians 4:17

✤*Hail Mary*✤

When people are saying, "Peace and security,"
then sudden disaster comes upon them, /
like labor pains upon a pregnant woman, and
they will not escape.

1 Thessalonians 5:3

✤*Hail Mary*✤

But you, brothers, are not in darkness, /
for that day to overtake you like a thief.

1 Thessalonians 5:4

✤*Hail Mary*✤

For God did not destine us for wrath, /
but to gain salvation through our Lord Jesus
Christ.

1 Thessalonians 5:9

✤*Hail Mary*✤

✤*Glory Be*✤

Fourth Parousia Mystery
The King Returns

✠*Our Father*✠

When the thousand years are completed, Satan
will be released from his prison. /
He will go out to deceive the nations at the four
corners of the earth . . .

Revelation 20:7-8

✠*Hail Mary*✠

Gog and Magog, to gather them for battle; /
their number is like the sand of the sea.

Revelation 20:8

✠*Hail Mary*✠

They invaded the breadth of the earth and
surrounded the camp of the holy ones and
the beloved city. /
But fire came down from heaven and consumed them.

Revelation 20:9

✠*Hail Mary*✠

The Devil who had led them astray was thrown
into the pool of fire and sulfur, where the
beast and the false prophet were. /
There they will be tormented day and night
forever and ever.

Revelation 20:10

✤Hail Mary✤

Next I saw a large white throne and the one who
was sitting on it. /
The earth and the sky fled from his presence and
there was no place for them.

Revelation 20:11

✤Hail Mary✤

I saw the dead, the great and the lowly, standing
before the throne, /
and scrolls were opened.

Revelation 20:12

✤Hail Mary✤

Then another scroll was opened, the book of life. /
The dead were judged according to their deeds,
by what was written in the scrolls.

Revelation 20:12

✤Hail Mary✤

The sea gave up its dead; then Death and Hades
gave up their dead. /
All the dead were judged according to their deeds.

Revelation 20:13

✤Hail Mary✤

Then Death and Hades were thrown into the pool
of fire. /

(This pool of fire is the second death.)

Revelation 20:14

✤Hail Mary✤

Anyone whose name was not found written in
the book of life /
was thrown into the pool of fire.

Revelation 20:15

✤Hail Mary✤

✤Glory Be✤

Fifth Parousia Mystery
The New Jerusalem

✤Our Father✤

Then I saw a new heaven and a new earth. /
The former heaven and the former earth had
passed away, and the sea was no more.

Revelation 21:1

✤Hail Mary✤

I also saw the holy city, a new Jerusalem,
coming down out of heaven from God, /
prepared as a bride adorned for her husband.

Revelation 21:2

✤Hail Mary✤

129

I heard a loud voice from the throne saying,
"Behold, God's dwelling is with the human
race. /

He will dwell with them and they will be his
people and God himself will always be with
them [as their God]."

Revelation 21:3

❖Hail Mary❖

"He will wipe every tear from their eyes, and
there shall be no more death or mourning,
wailing or pain, /

[for] the old order has passed away."

Revelation 21:4

❖Hail Mary❖

The one who sat on the throne said, "Behold, I
make all things new. /

. . . To the thirsty I will give a gift from the
spring of life-giving water."

Revelation 21:5-6

❖Hail Mary❖

"The victor will inherit these gifts, and I shall be
his God, /

and he will be my son."

Revelation 21:7

❖Hail Mary❖

"But as for cowards, the unfaithful, the depraved, murderers, the unchaste, sorcerers, idol-worshipers, and deceivers of every sort, /

their lot is in the burning pool of fire and sulfur, which is the second death."

Revelation 21:8

✤Hail Mary✤

"Behold, I am coming soon. I bring with me the recompense /

I will give to each according to his deeds."

Revelation 22:12

✤Hail Mary✤

Blessed are they who wash their robes so as to have the right to the tree of life /

and enter the city through its gates.

Revelation 22:14

✤Hail Mary✤

The one who gives this testimony says, "Yes, I am coming soon." /

Amen! Come, Lord Jesus!

Revelation 22:20

✤Hail Mary✤

✤Glory Be✤

Appendix A
Prayers of the Rosary

APOSTLES' CREED

I believe in God, the Father almighty, Creator of heaven and earth; and in Jesus Christ, his only Son, our Lord; who was conceived by the Holy Spirit, born of the Virgin Mary; suffered under Pontius Pilate, was crucified, died, and was buried. He descended into hell; the third day he arose again from the dead. He ascended into heaven, and is seated at the right hand of God the Father almighty; from thence he shall come to judge the living and the dead. I believe in the Holy Spirit, the Holy Catholic Church, the Communion of Saints, the forgiveness of sins, the resurrection of the body, and life everlasting. Amen.

OUR FATHER

Our Father, who art in heaven, hallowed be thy name. Thy kingdom come. Thy will be done, on earth as it is in heaven. Give us this day our daily bread; and forgive us our trespasses as we forgive those who trespass against us; and lead us not into temptation, but deliver us from evil. Amen.

HAIL MARY

Hail Mary, full of grace, the Lord is with thee; blessed art thou among women, and blessed is the fruit of thy womb, Jesus. Holy Mary, Mother of God, pray for us sinners, now and at the hour of our death. Amen.

GLORY BE

Glory be to the Father, and to the Son, and to the Holy Spirit; as it was in the beginning, is now, and ever shall be, world without end. Amen.

FATIMA PRAYER

O my Jesus, forgive us our sins, save us from the fires of hell, and lead all souls to heaven, especially those most in need of thy mercy. *(Note: Commonly prayed after each Glory Be.)*

HAIL HOLY QUEEN

Hail, Holy Queen, Mother of mercy! Hail, our life, our sweetness, and our hope! To thee do we cry, poor banished children of Eve; to thee do we send up our sighs, mourning and weeping in this valley of tears! Turn then, most gracious advocate, thine eyes of mercy toward us; and after this, our exile, show unto us the blessed fruit of thy womb, Jesus. O clement, O loving, O sweet Virgin Mary!

(Note: It is very fitting to say the Hail Holy Queen at the end of the Rosary.)

Appendix B
How to Pray the Rosary

1. After making the Sign of the Cross, say the Apostles' Creed.

2. Say the Our Father.

3. Say three Hail Marys.

4. Say the Glory Be to the Father.

5. Announce the first mystery, then say the Our Father.

6. Read the first Scripture excerpt, then say the first Hail Mary while meditating on the mystery.

7. Repeat step 6 for the nine remaining Hail Marys in the decade.

8. Say the Glory Be to the Father.

9. Announce the second mystery, then say the Our Father. Repeat steps 6, 7, and 8 and continue with the third, fourth, and fifth mysteries in the same manner.

10. While not essential, it is very fitting to say the Hail Holy Queen at the end of the Rosary, then kiss the cross and make the Sign of the Cross